W9-ARF-123

Foods of Indonesia

Barbara Sheen

KIDHAVEN PRESS
A part of Gale, Cengage Learning

Detroit • New York • San Francisco • New Haven, Conn • Waterville, Maine • London

© 2012 Gale, Cengage Learning

ALL RIGHTS RESERVED. No part of this work covered by the copyright herein may be reproduced, transmitted, stored, or used in any form or by any means graphic, electronic, or mechanical, including but not limited to photocopying, recording, scanning, digitizing, taping, Web distribution, information networks, or information storage and retrieval systems, except as permitted under Section 107 or 108 of the 1976 United States Copyright Act, without the prior written permission of the publisher.

Every effort has been made to trace the owners of copyrighted material.

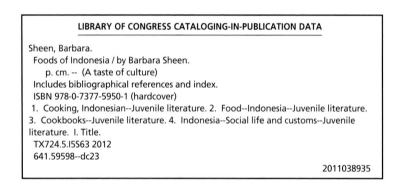

LIBRARY OF CONGRESS CATALOGING-IN-PUBLICATION DATA

Sheen, Barbara.
  Foods of Indonesia / by Barbara Sheen.
    p. cm. -- (A taste of culture)
  Includes bibliographical references and index.
  ISBN 978-0-7377-5950-1 (hardcover)
  1. Cooking, Indonesian--Juvenile literature. 2. Food--Indonesia--Juvenile literature. 3. Cookbooks--Juvenile literature. 4. Indonesia--Social life and customs--Juvenile literature. I. Title.
  TX724.5.I5S63 2012
  641.59598--dc23
                                                              2011038935

Kidhaven Press
27500 Drake Rd.
Farmington Hills MI 48331

ISBN-13: 978-0-7377-5950-1
ISBN-10: 0-7377-5950-X

Printed in the United States of America
1 2 3 4 5 6 7 15 14 13 12 11

Contents

A Special Place

With its green jungles perfumed by spices, its cone-shaped volcanoes covered in mist, its white sandy beaches and turquoise waters, Indonesia is a special place. Indonesia is the world's largest **archipelago** (ark-ih-PELL-uh-go), or string of islands. The country consists of more than 17,000 tropical islands, but people live on only 6,000 of them. These islands are scattered on both sides of the equator, between the continents of Asia and Australia. In total, the islands cover an area of about 741,000 square miles (1.9 million square km). The islands' warm climate, rich volcanic soil, lush vegetation, and cool coastal waters provide plenty of food. Tropical fruit, nuts, meat, and

FOOD REGIONS OF INDONESIA

Cattle
Chicken
Coconut
Coffee
Corn
Fish
Goat
Palm Oil
Rice
Sheep
Sweet Potato
Vegetables

poultry are all part of Indonesian cooking. But it is the spices, chili peppers, rice, seafood, and vegetables that Indonesian cooks cannot do without. These ingredients make Indonesian cooking as colorful and fragrant as the islands themselves.

Spicy Jewels

Traders have journeyed to Indonesia seeking spices since ancient times. These strong-smelling, flavorful seasonings have often been considered more valuable than jewels. Indonesia's history and development are closely linked to the spice trade. It brought wealth and contact with other cultures to the islands, but it also brought conflict. One of the greatest values of Indonesian spices—both in years past and today—is the flavor they add to cooking on the islands.

Nutmeg, cloves, cinnamon, ginger, pepper, and a

A bowl of sambal.

About Indonesia

Indonesia has about 242 million people. That makes Indonesia the world's fourth most populous nation. It also has more Muslims than any other nation. Java is Indonesia's largest island. It is one of the most densely populated places on Earth. Other large islands include Sumatra, Sulawesi, Bali, Kalimantan, and the Moluccas.

Indonesia divides the Pacific and Indian Oceans. It is located on the ring of fire. This is the name of the region with many volcanoes and frequent earthquakes. Indonesia has the world's largest number of active volcanoes.

The climate is hot. There are two seasons, rainy and dry. Crops are harvested year round. Important crops include spices, rice, cocoa, coffee, peanuts, tea, and rubber. Indonesia also produces lumber, natural gas, oil, tin, coal, copper, nickel, and gold. It is Southeast Asia's largest exporter of oil, and the world's largest exporter of liquefied natural gas.

bitter orange spice called turmeric (TER-muh-rick) are just a few of the spices native to Indonesia. In fact, for a long time Indonesia was the only place in the world where nutmeg and cloves grew. Other spices arrived with the Chinese and Arab traders. Sixteenth-century Portuguese sailors brought chili peppers to Indonesia from Latin America.

With so many spices to choose from, Indonesian cooks rarely use just one in their cooking. They mash a variety of fresh spices together, then **sauté** (saw-

TAY) them in oil to make a creamy flavoring paste known as **bumbu-bumbu** (BOOM-boo-BOOM-boo). Roots, pods, seeds, and leaves of whole spices are often added. So is **palm sugar**, which is a type of brown sugar made from the sap of palm trees. Also added to bumbu-bumbu is shrimp paste. This is a tangy paste made of dried shrimp. A few tablespoons of **coconut milk** turns the paste into a rich sauce. The amounts and combinations of spices in bumbu-bumbu vary from dish to dish, island to island, and cook to cook. The goal is to improve the flavor and scent of the food, not make it fiery hot. These pastes, according to food writer and author James Oseland, "are the soul of a dish, the palette from which the cook determines how pungent, aromatic, earthy, or sour it will be."[1]

Spices are also used to make **sambal,** a brightly colored **condiment** that is similar to relish and is served with every meal. There are many different varieties of sambal, but the foundation of all of them is chili peppers. Hundreds of different types of chili peppers grow in Indonesia. Almost any type can be used in sambal. The pepper's heat is balanced by sweet, sour, and salty ingredients, such as green mango, onions, garlic, lime juice, and shrimp paste. Indonesians put sambal on rice, fish, meat, and vegetables. "A meal," explains Josephine Chua, an Indonesian architect, "would be unthinkable without it."[2]

A Valuable Nut

Coconuts are an important part of the Indonesian diet. The nutmeat adds sweetness, chewiness, and valuable nutrients to many dishes. One coconut has more protein than a steak. Coconut milk is a liquid that is made by mixing grated coconut with water. In Indonesia coconut milk is an important ingredient in sauces. Coconut juice, the clear sweet liquid found in the center of coconuts, is a popular drink. Coconut oil is a common cooking oil in Indonesia. It is also an ingredient in shampoos and skin lotions.

The coconut palm tree is useful, too. In the past, the flowers were used to make shoes and caps. Even today, the leaves are woven into furnishings. Coconut shells are often carved and used as platters. They are also ground up and used to make plastic. The roots are used to make mouthwash, treatments for stomach illnesses, and dye.

An Indonesian boy drinks juice from a coconut.

A Perfect Complement

Rice, with its snow-white color and mild flavor, is a perfect complement to bumbu-bumbu and sambal. Indonesians have been growing rice for at least 3,000 years. Rice paddies snake down Indonesian hillsides, border beaches and jungles, and blanket the countryside in bright shades of green. Indonesia is one of the world's largest growers and consumers of rice. Rice production is the main source of income for about 100 million Indonesians. Rice is also the centerpiece of every meal. "Wherever you turn, rice is there shaping the landscape, sold at markets, hidden in sweets and piled on your plate,"[3] says author Patrick Witton.

Terraced rice fields in Bali.

Coconut Rice

Cooking rice in coconut milk gives the rice a delicate and exotic taste and fragrance.

Ingredients
1 cup long grain white rice
1 can (14 ounces) coconut milk
1 ¼ cup water
1 tablespoon melted butter
Pinch salt

Directions
1. Combine all the ingredients in a large pot. Bring to a boil over medium heat.
2. Reduce heat to low. Cover the pot. Cook until the rice is fluffy and the liquid is absorbed, about 20 minutes.

Serves 4.

Coconut rice with mango slices.

Indonesians eat about 440 pounds (200kg) of rice per person each year. In comparison, Americans eat about 20 pounds (44kg) in a year. A typical Indonesian meal consists of a large bowl of rice placed in the center of the table, surrounded by smaller bowls of sambal, meat, vegetables, and fish. These foods often are cooked in spicy sauces. Diners scoop a mound of rice onto their plates. They top it with a few morsels of meat, fish, and/or vegetables, and a bit of sambal. Author Rafael Steinberg explains: "Rice … is the main course, the essential element in every meal. The housewife buys rice first and plans her meal around it."[4]

Since Indonesians traditionally eat with their fingers, rice also serves as an eating utensil. When topped with a small amount of sauce it becomes sticky enough to mold into a little ball, which diners then pop into their mouths

Fish and Other Seafood

Delicious dishes made with fresh fish or other seafood are often served with the rice. Indonesia is surrounded by water, and there are many inland waterways as well. Therefore, **edible** water creatures are almost everywhere. Even flooded rice

Local Indonesian women sell fish at a market.

paddies are home to fish. And, fishing is a way for millions of Indonesians to make money.

Fish and other seafood just pulled from Indonesia's warm waters are the Indonesian people's main source of protein. Tuna, salmon, sardines, catfish, red snapper, and shrimp are just a few of the many seafood choices, but only the freshest will do. Cooks buy live fish right off of fishing boats. Many cooks keep their purchase alive in a bucket of water until they are ready to cook it. Indonesians steam whole fish with herbs and spices. They wrap fish in banana leaves and grill it over hot coals. They deep-fry it and serve it with a hot sauce. They dry

shrimp to make shrimp paste, and they fry shrimp with flour and eggs to form crunchy, puffy crackers. "From [the Indonesian cities of] Sabang to Merauke there'll be ikan (fish). … This is the dietary constant across the archipelago,"[5] Witton explains.

Gifts of Nature

Indonesia's fertile soil produces a mind-boggling variety of vegetables and edible green leafy vegetables. Many grow wild. Others are grown on farms, in little gardens, and anywhere there is space, including between the buildings on university campuses and on vacant lots in the cities. Food writer Oseland recalls: "On my first trip to Jakarta [Indonesia's capital], I was amazed by the fields of vegetables that thrived right next to busy streets. Women in sarongs [long pieces of cloth that is worn as a skirt or dress] busily picking red chilis and eggplants as jeeps sped past nearby."[6]

Indonesian markets overflow with freshly picked vegetables. Some, like potatoes, corn, carrots, bean sprouts, and onions, are well known in North America. Others are less familiar. There are 40 different varieties of a mildly flavored cabbage called bok choy. There also are greens, like sour lime leaves and Kangkung (KANG-koong). Kangkung is a spinach-like leaf vegetable that grows in ditches and swamps. There are multicolored dried beans, long green beans, tiny thumb-sized eggplants, and fat yellow-skinned cucumbers. The list goes on and on.

Two or three vegetable dishes are served with al-

Stir-Fried Greens

Indonesians enjoy lightly cooked greens. This recipe uses bok choy, but any greens can be used instead. Indonesians usually fry foods in peanut or coconut oil. Sesame oil or other vegetable oils can also be used.

Ingredients
1 pound bok choy
2 tablespoons peanut oil
1 teaspoon red pepper flakes
1 teaspoon minced garlic
1 teaspoon ginger
pinch salt

Directions
1. Wash the bok choy. Cut off the bottom. Slice the bok choy into about 3-inch pieces.
2. Heat the oil in a deep pan over medium heat. When the oil is hot, add all the ingredients. Cook the greens for about 3–5 minutes, stirring constantly until the greens are wilted but not limp.

Serves 4.

most every meal. They may be cold or hot, fresh or pickled, plain or flavored with spices and delicious sauces. Greens that are fried in peanut oil with sliced chili and splashed with soy sauce is a popular dish with rice. So are mixed vegetables simmered in spiced coconut milk. Most cooks visit vegetable markets every day in search of the freshest, tastiest vegetables and leafy greens. They touch, smell, and snap off little pieces to check for quality and freshness.

Near-perfect choices are not hard to find. With vegetables, leafy greens, rice, and spices growing almost everywhere, and waters overflowing with seafood, Indonesia is truly blessed with a rich food supply. Indonesian cooks delight in their choices. No matter what other ingredients are used, fresh seafood, brightly colored chili peppers, aromatic spices, vegetables, and snow-white rice hold a special place in their kitchen. They are an important part of what makes Indonesia such a special place.

Chapter 2

Unity in Diversity

Indonesia's national slogan is "Unity in Diversity." This means that all types of people can come together in one united country. Indeed, Indonesia is made up of many different types of people. In fact, Indonesians represent more than 300 ethnic groups and speak as many languages. The first people in Indonesia were settlers from Southeast Asia, China, and Polynesia. Next came foreign traders and invaders from India, Arabia, Portugal, England, Holland, and Japan. The distance between the islands that make up Indonesia also add to the differences among its people. Favorite dishes like nasi goreng (NAH-see GOR-eg), gado-gado (GAH-doh GAH-doh), satay (SAH-tay), and rendang

(REN-deg) are a product of Indonesia's diverse population, many islands, and the different groups who have been a part of its history.

Fried Rice

Nasi goreng is fried rice, which is often made from left-over rice. It is Indonesia's national dish and is eaten at elegant dinner parties, as a snack, and as a popular breakfast food in Indonesia.

Nasi goreng can contain any number of ingredients. There are probably as many versions as there are Indonesian cooks. In its most basic form, nasi goreng consists of white rice that is stir-fried in oil with garlic and red chilis. The mixture is flavored with **kecap manis** (KEH-chahp MAH-nees). This sauce is a sweet and

A fried egg tops a portion of nasi goreng.

A Stormy History

Indonesia's earliest people are called Java Men. Historians think they came to Indonesia over a land bridge from Asia around 1 million years ago. People from China and Southeast Asia traveled to Indonesia over thousands of years. By the 7th century B.C. Indonesia had become an advanced civilization. Its location on the sea lanes between India and China brought traders from these countries and from Arabia.

European traders fought for control of Indonesia in order to capture Indonesia's spice trade. In 1511 the Portuguese seized most of Indonesia and ruled there for almost 100 years. In 1605 the Dutch overthrew the Portuguese. Except for a brief period from 1811–1816 when the British gained control, the Dutch ruled Indonesia until 1945. The Japanese occupied Indonesia during World War II. Indonesia finally became an independent nation in 1945.

salty mixture of soy sauce and palm sugar. It is the food item from which the common condiment ketchup gets its name.

Nasi goreng can contain shrimp, fish, mixed vegetables, different flavored pastes, and meat or poultry. It is always served with a fried egg on top, and is usually served with sambal, crunchy shrimp crackers, and cool fresh cucumber slices.

The dish was brought to Indonesia by the Chinese. Indonesian cooks added personal touches, island by island. On the island of Sumatra, for example, salty anchovies are added, while on Java palm sugar sweetens the rice. No matter the recipe, nasi goreng has a satisfying, earthy taste, a delightful mixture of flavors, and an exotic aroma. Upon tasting a batch while filming in Indonesia, chef and Travel Channel host Anthony Bourdain declared, "This stuff is great!"[7] Most Indonesians would agree.

Meat, Spices, and Coconut Milk

Rendang is another popular dish. Rendang is a type of curry. *Curry* is a term that describes any number of stew-like dishes in which meat, chicken, fish, or vegetables are cooked in a spicy sauce. Spices help preserve foods. The more heavily a food is spiced, the longer it can keep without refrigeration. The practice

A customer in Pandang waits for her food to be served from the display window.

of using curry to keep meat from spoiling first started in India. It was brought to Indonesia by first-century Indian merchants. Indonesian cooks soon developed their own curry recipes. Rendang is among the most popular.

Rendang is made by slowly cooking meat in spices and coconut milk until the sauce almost disappears. What is left thickens, enveloping the meat with a dense, very spicy, dark-red coating. Different spices may be used in making the sauce. Fiery-hot red chilis, lime leaves, **cumin** (COO-min), **coriander** (COR-ee-an-der), nutmeg, and cloves are usually part of the mixture. The meat, too, can be almost any kind. Pork, however, is rarely used. Most Indonesians are Muslims and their religion does not allow them to eat pork. On the island of Bali, most of the people believe in the Hindu religion. Here, beef is not used because Hinduism forbids the eating of beef.

Water buffalo rendang is a traditional favorite. The meat of a water buffalo is tough, but slowly cooking it makes it melt-in-the-mouth tender. Chicken, goat, shrimp, and fish are also used in rendang. No matter the main ingredient, rendang is eaten by all Indonesians. It is a specialty of Pandang, a town on the island of Sumatra that is famous for its very spicy food. Pandang -style cooking is so popular in Indonesia that there are Pandang restaurants in almost every Indonesian town. Dining in Pandang restaurants is an interesting experience. The food is cooked ahead of time and displayed

Delicious Fruit

Indonesians love fruit. Some of the most popular fruits, such as avocados, water-melons, mangoes, pineapple, and bananas, are familiar to North Americans. Others, like pomelos, are not. Pomelos are citrus fruits that look like extra-large grapefruit but taste much sweeter. Spiky-skinned, football-shaped durians are even less well-known. When they are cut open, they give off a strong odor that many people dislike. Despite the odor, the fruit inside has a sweet custard-like flavor that many people love.

Other favorite fruits are not so sweet. Soursops have bumpy green skin and are tart like a lemon. Tamarinds are another sour fruit. They are used to add tartness in flavoring pastes and sauces.

Jackfruit is the largest fruit in the world, A single jackfruit can weigh up to 100 pounds (45.36 kilograms). Indonesians turn jackfruit into preserves, use it in cooking, and eat it fresh. It tastes a little like a banana.

Jackfruits are transported by bicycle through the streets.

in the front windows. The food sits for many hours, but because it is very spicy, it does not spoil. There is no menu in Pandang restaurants. Instead, waiters bring out a large bowl of rice and dozens of smaller bowls of different foods, including rendang. Diners eat what they like and when they are finished, the waiter takes away the untouched bowls and counts the number of empty bowls to figure out the bill. "You don't need to order," Bourdain explains. "[Pandang chefs] just bring out everything they have. … Sample any dish you like along with rice…. Then they just count the dishes. You can identify these restaurants by the pyramid of food in the window."[8]

Sizzling Meat on a Stick

Satay is meat or fish that is threaded onto a stick called a skewer and cooked over an open fire. Satay is probably the most famous of all Indonesian dishes. Satay is similar to Arab skewered-meat dishes known as kebabs. Invaders from the Middle East introduced this type of food to Indonesia in the 13th century. They also brought the Muslim religion to Indonesia at that time.

Satay recipes differ from island to island. Indonesians make 29 different types of satay. Most of them are named for the region from which they come. Despite regional variations, all satays have a lot in common. The meat can be beef, chicken, goat, lamb, fish, or shrimp, but it is always soaked in a spicy sauce. Then it is threaded on small, sharp, thin skewers and grilled until it is brown on the outside and tender and juicy

Men cooking satay over an open fire.

on the inside. Traditionally, the skewers are made of bamboo or from the center rib of a coconut palm leaf. Coconut palm skewers add a nutty, sweet flavor to the grilled meat.

The cooking itself is done over a small rectangular grill that is usually fueled with bits of coconut shell. As the shells burn, they fill the air with an exotic sweet-smelling smoke. At the same time, they scent and flavor the meat. According to an Indonesian man named Karma, the coconut shells "flavor the meat with the tropics."[9]

The hot, juicy meat is served with sambal and various sweet-and-spicy dipping sauces. Peanut sauce is especially popular. Richly scented rice cakes steamed in banana leaves and pickled cucumbers known as acar are commonly served with satay. The result is incredibly fragrant and meltingly tender. Satay is layered with different flavors: smoky, earthy, sweet, zesty, and totally delicious.

Indonesian Salad

Gado-gado means hodgepodge or mixture in Indonesian. It is another popular dish. This Indonesian salad originated on the island of Java. It contains many ingredients that were brought to Indonesia by the different groups that came to live there. Although almost any vegetable can be used and ingredients vary on different islands, the salad usually contains potatoes, cabbage, and **tofu**, or soybean curd. Potatoes were brought to Indonesia by the Portuguese, cabbage came to Indone-

Shrimp Satay

Satay can be made with shrimp, scallops, fish, chicken, beef, or pork. It can be cooked on a grill, in a pan, or in a broiler.

Ingredients
1 pound large shrimp, peeled and deveined
3 tablespoons soy sauce
1 tablespoon fresh lime juice
1 tablespoon peanut oil
1 teaspoon crushed red pepper
1 teaspoon minced garlic
1 teaspoon ginger
1 teaspoon honey
12 bamboo skewers, soaked in water overnight

Directions
1. Mix all the ingredients except the shrimp together in a bowl or a self-closing plastic bag. Add the shrimp to the mixture. Refrigerate for at least 1 hour.
2. Remove the shrimp from the sauce. Thread the shrimp through the skewers. Grill on high heat until the shrimp are cooked through, about 5 minutes.

Serves 4.

Shrimp satay.

Peanut Sauce

Satay is usually served with peanut sauce for dipping. The sauce is also served with salads, chicken, fish, tofu, and tempeh. For a less-creamy sauce use chunky peanut butter.

Ingredients
½ cup creamy peanut butter
½ cup unsweetened coconut milk
¼ cup water
1 tablespoon brown sugar
1 tablespoon soy sauce
1 tablespoon fresh lime juice
1 teaspoon crushed red pepper
½ teaspoon ground ginger

Directions
1. Combine all the ingredients in a microwave-safe bowl. Mix well to form a smooth sauce.
2. Microwave for two minutes.

Serves 2–4.

sia with the Dutch, and tofu arrived with the Chinese. Other ingredients include both raw and lightly cooked greens, bean sprouts, cucumber, carrots, green beans, and sliced hard-boiled eggs, to name a few. The whole thing is topped with a spicy, creamy peanut sauce and crunchy shrimp crackers.

Like its name, gado-gado is a true jumble of colors, textures, aromas, and flavors. "Everybody does

A bowl of gado-gado salad with peanut sauce.

it slightly differently," says Indonesian chef William Wongso. "That's the beauty. You can have it how you like it."[10]

Indonesians are creative with all their favorite dishes. The distances that separate the islands and the many ethnic groups that call Indonesia home have had an effect on Indonesian cooking. Yet, despite regional differences, all of Indonesia's favorite dishes share many common characteristics. They especially help tie Indonesians together, creating unity in diversity.

Chapter 3

A Flavorful Adventure

Indonesia's streets are a flavorful adventure. Its cities, towns, and roadsides are packed with food vendors who sell almost every kind of Indonesian food and drink. Vendors known as **kaki-limas** (KAH-khee-LEE-mahs) push colorful three-wheeled carts that contain a little stove, a workbench, and a cabinet that holds the ingredients. *Kaki-lima* means five legs, which is the sum of "legs" when adding the vendor's two legs and the three wheels on the cart. Other vendors set up canvas-covered food stalls called **warungs** (WAH-ruhngs). A warung is a folding eatery with a portable kitchen and long tables and benches. Warungs have specific hours, and are set up and taken down at the start and close

Because of their portability, warungs can be found on Indonesian beaches.

of each day. Eating at a warung is a social activity. Everyone from businesspeople to small children share a table. Visiting with fellow diners is part of the fun.

Food vendors have their own specialties that they advertise on colorful handmade signs. Many are famous for their cooking that draws customers from miles around. Nights are especially busy. According to author Patrick Witton, "[Parking lots], footpaths and intersections are crammed with eateries, filling the evening air with the smells and sounds of stir frying. … There's always another stall just around the corner. … Hungry or not, you'll be tempted by strange foods, waylaid by exotic aromas and entranced [delighted] by new flavors."[11]

Indonesian Handicrafts

Indonesia is famous for its handicrafts. Indonesian batik cloth, in particular, is world famous. Batik is a method of creating designs on cloth using dye and wax. First the removable wax is placed at different places on the fabric; then the cloth is dipped into dye. The wax is then removed and the cloth becomes colored in the areas where the wax was not applied.

Indonesian wood carvings are also famous, as is the country's jewelry. Indonesia has many pearl farms, where oysters are raised for pearls. These farms produce large amounts of pearls that are then turned into jewelry.

Other crafted items tell stories, such as carved masks that are worn by traditional dancers, and wood-and-leather shadow puppets. Areas on these flat puppets are cut out to create facial features and other details. The puppets are placed behind a see-through screen with a light shining on them from behind. As the puppeteer moves the long rods attached to the puppets, the audience sees the moving shadows on the other side of the screen.

A puppeter uses traditional shadow puppets to entertain young children.

Savory Treats

Cooks prepare hundreds of different kinds of savory treats. Bakso (BAHK-so) is a meatball noodle soup that may very well be the Indonesian people's favorite dish. "When people hang out at night and they feel hungry, they go for bakso,"[12] says Indonesian chef Djoko Supatmono.

Bakso recipes vary, because all cooks add their own special touches. For instance, any kind of ground meat mixed with herbs and spices can be used to make the meatballs. The bakso range in size from as small as golf balls to as large as tennis balls. Some cooks hide a boiled egg inside the meatballs. The noodles also vary. They can be made from wheat, rice, or bean flour. Whatever else goes into the soup is up to the cook. Vegetables, greens, chunks of crispy fried tofu, steamed and fried dumplings, and fried onions are popular ingredients. No matter the recipe, the result is a rich soup filled with layers of flavor, texture, and color.

Other savory treats are fried foods. Fried chicken, which is first boiled in coconut milk to sweeten and soften it, is a top choice. So are fried catfish and fried **tempeh** (TEM-pay). Tempeh is made from cooked soybeans that are sprinkled with yeast and wrapped in banana leaves. The leaf-covered soybeans are then left for two days to become sour. During this time, harmless bacteria fill the spaces between the beans, turning the mixture into a soft but solid, nut-flavored block that is healthy.

A bowl of bakso, a traditional Indonesian soup.

Vendors cut slices off the block and fry them in hot oil until the tempeh is crisp and golden. Then, they pour sweet-and-spicy sauce on top. Vendors also fry plantains, which are long green bananas that are eaten like vegetables. They turn corn and potatoes into deep-fried patties or fritters. Most fried treats are served with fresh sambal and cucumber slices. The cucumber's fresh, clean taste perfectly balances the richness of the fried foods.

Sweet Treats

Plenty of sweet treats are eaten in Indonesia. In fact, Indonesians eat them day and night. They say that eating sweets is a way to celebrate the sweetness of life. Food writer James Oseland explains:

> The people of Indonesia … are passionate about their kueh-kueh, or sweets. They're an essential part of everyday life and they're

Fried Tempeh

Tempeh is sold in many supermarkets, health food stores, and Asian markets. If tempeh is unavailable, tofu can be substituted. This dish tastes good served with rice.

Ingredients

1 pound tempeh, cut into ½-inch cubes
2–3 tablespoons peanut oil
1 small white onion, sliced
¼ cup soy sauce
2 tablespoons water
1 tomato, chopped
1 tablespoon brown sugar
1 teaspoon minced garlic
1 teaspoon crushed red pepper

Directions

1. Combine the soy sauce, sugar, red pepper, and water.
2. Heat the oil in a deep frying pan or wok. Add the onion and garlic, fry until the onions are soft. Add the tempeh, tomato, and sauce. Fry, stirring constantly until the tempeh is golden about 3 minutes.

Serves 4.

eaten throughout the day, not just paraded out after dinner or on special occasions. For many people in the region, especially residents of Java and Bali, sweets are powerful symbols. They represent the riches the world has to offer. ... I can't recall ever going into someone's home and not being welcomed with a slice of freshly baked cake or a sticky rice treat—with something, anything sweet.[13]

Many sweets contain rice. Onde onde (ON-day ON-day) are delectable dumplings made of rice flour and coconut milk, and filled with palm sugar. The little balls are dropped into boiling water. As they cook, the filling melts into caramel syrup. While they are still warm, the dumplings are rolled in plates of shredded coconut. Upon taking a bite, the syrup bursts out, blending with the delicate pastry and the fresh coconut. The flavor is nutty, exotic, and sweet.

Yummy pancakes known as serabi (SRAH-bee) are also made with rice flour and coconut milk. These pancakes are flavored with pandan, which is an herb that smells and tastes like vanilla, They are then topped with chocolate or sliced bananas. Soft, sweet, aromatic, and fluffy, "they're just remarkable little pillows of goodness,"[14] says chef and TV host Anthony Bourdain.

An Indonesian girl holding a sticky rice ball.

A Favorite Candy

Indonesians love candy. Dodol (DOH-dohl) is one of their favorites. It is caramel candy made with rice flour, sugar, and coconut milk. It takes a lot of effort to make dodol. The ingredients are cooked for up to nine hours. The mixture must be stirred the whole time it is cooking or it will not turn out smooth. The dodol is done when the ingredients become firm and no longer stick to the cook's fingers when touched. The candy is then placed into a big pan to cool. Finally, it is cut into little pieces and wrapped in colorful paper.

Dodol is similar to taffy in that it is very sweet and has a chewy, almost rubbery, texture. It is sold all over Indonesia and is available in different flavors, including coconut, apple, soursop, and jackfruit. It is eaten year-round and is also a popular treat during holidays and festivals.

Delicious Beverages

Other vendors sell delicious drinks, including coffee, tea, coconut water, and fruit drinks. Indonesia is the world's third-largest coffee grower. Coffee plantations dot the islands of Bali, Sumatra, Sulawesi, and, especially, Java, which may be why *java* is a nickname for coffee in the United States. Indonesians grind their coffee beans coarsely so that the beverage has a slightly gritty taste. They drink their coffee hot and black and with lots of palm sugar. Coffee is also brewed with ginger, which gives it a warm spicy flavor. An even spicier coffee is made on the island of Sulawesi, where the beverage is sometimes brewed with roasted garlic.

Tea is even more popular than coffee in Indonesia. The Dutch first planted tea on the islands in the 17th century. Tea plantations are now a common sight in the volcanic highlands of Java and Sumatra. Sipping glasses of tea throughout the day is an essential part of Indonesian life. Tea is also the most common drink at mealtime. Indonesians prefer their tea much like their coffee: strongly flavored and with lots of sugar but no cream. They often mix jasmine flowers in with the tea leaves, which makes the drink smell like a tropical garden. On some islands a cinnamon stick is added to the

Indonesian men drink tea in a back street shop.

water that the tea is brewed in. The cinnamon gives the beverage a warm, earthy scent and flavor.

Tea is served both hot and iced. Iced drinks are very refreshing in Indonesia's hot climate. One popular iced drink is known as apokat (AH-poh-kaht). It is a rich, thick, avocado smoothie that is flavored with either coffee or chocolate syrup, or both. The idea of using avocados to make a sweet drink might seem strange to North Americans who usually eat avocados the way they do vegetables. But an avocado is actually a fruit that mixes well with sweet ingredients. Pepy, the author of an Indonesian cooking blog, explains:

> For people who only know that avocado is added into [a] savory dish, I'll tell you something about avocado. I grew up with fresh fruit shakes that we can buy from the street food hawkers at most places in Indonesia. My favorite fruit shakes are guava, soursop [similar to a lemon] and avocado. … Yes, an avocado . . . shake is a very popular beverage in Indonesia. … Every family or person has their own recipe. My family used to add coffee … and chocolate, sweetened condensed milk or mocha [coffee-flavored] syrup. … Some people serve this with ice cream on top and it's called [an] avocado float.[15]

Other favorite beverages include juices and shakes, cordials, and coconut water. The juices and shakes are

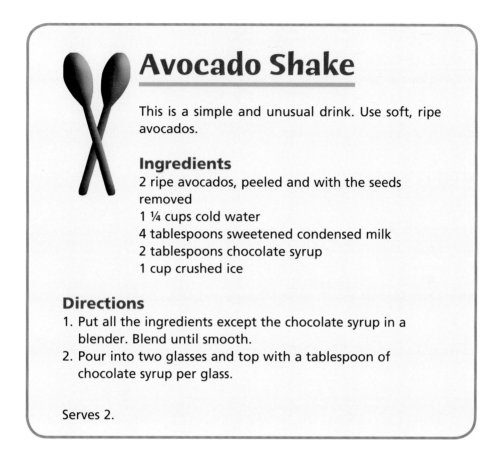

Avocado Shake

This is a simple and unusual drink. Use soft, ripe avocados.

Ingredients

2 ripe avocados, peeled and with the seeds removed
1 ¼ cups cold water
4 tablespoons sweetened condensed milk
2 tablespoons chocolate syrup
1 cup crushed ice

Directions

1. Put all the ingredients except the chocolate syrup in a blender. Blend until smooth.
2. Pour into two glasses and top with a tablespoon of chocolate syrup per glass.

Serves 2.

made with freshly squeezed fruit. Cordials are made with plain or sparkling water and fruit syrup. Coconut water is the clear, sweet liquid found inside a coconut. Vendors slice the tops off coconuts with a hatchet-like tool, and thirsty Indonesians drink the liquid right from the shell.

Strolling down an Indonesian street is a flavorful adventure. The air is filled with enticing aromas, and there is something mouthwatering around every corner. It is hard to resist stopping for an icy beverage or a sweet or savory bite.

Beautiful Food

Indonesian cooks try to tempt all the senses. They use different colors, shapes, textures, and fragrances to make Indonesian cooking interesting. "Food is really pretty here," explains chef and Travel Channel host Anthony Bourdain. "Just the very act of eating here is amazing. The colors are out of this world. The spices, the condiments, the little things like the tiny plates of spicy red chilis, the smells and sounds of sizzling food over charcoal all play a part."[16] Special foods that are beautiful, fragrant, and delicious are an important part of Indonesian celebrations.

A Golden Rice Pyramid

A banquet, or selamatan (SLAH-mah-than), in which dozens of dishes are served is the Indonesian people's favorite way to celebrate marriages, births, anniversaries, and other happy events. A golden rice pyramid known as tumpeng is usually the centerpiece of the celebration.

A tumpeng is a sight to behold. It is a perfectly shaped inverted cone of rice that is cooked in coconut milk, perfumed with lemon, ginger, and vanilla-scented spices, and tinted bright gold with turmeric. The cone is topped with bright-red chili peppers, and its sides are covered in nuts, vegetables, and/or scrambled eggs. Tumpeng is surrounded by dozens of

Tumpengs line a table during a ceremonial meal.

small dishes filled with sambal, fried chicken, chicken cooked in coconut milk, liver cooked with chilis, vegetables, and fried tempeh, to name a few.

The tumpeng's shape looks like that of an Indonesian volcano, which was sacred to ancient Indonesians. Its golden color symbolizes good luck and wealth. To form it, Indonesian cooks use a special cone-shaped bamboo mold. Tumpeng can be any size, from a few inches to many feet tall. In the past huge tumpengs were specially created for holy days. They were placed on a huge platter and carried through the center of Indonesian towns followed by a long line of people. These tumpengs were so massive that it took eight men to carry just one cone.

No matter its size, tumpeng is impressive to see and to taste. Author Rafael Steinberg recalls a selamatan he attended in Indonesia:

> The first thing that caught my eye as I entered the room was a foot-high cone of steamed rice dominating [covering] one of the tables. Long green beans decorated the sides of this tumpeng and a bright red chili pepper had been stuck in the top of it pointing up. The cone stood in the center of a flat bamboo basket surrounded by symmetrical fields of small fried salted fish, boiled eggs, fried soybean curd, mung bean sprouts and numerous boiled vegetables mixed with spiced grated coconut. Although designed for

Indonesian Meals

Indonesians eat throughout the day. Although families often eat together, it is also common for people to snack on small dishes whenever they are hungry. Indonesian cooks prepare all of the day's food in the morning. This is likely to include a large pot of rice, fresh sambal, and a few fish, meat, and/or vegetable dishes. The rice is kept warm in a rice cooker. Since most Indonesians do not have refrigerators, the rest of the food is covered and left on the table for family members to eat whenever they like. The spices in the food keep it from spoiling. Except for the rice, food is eaten at room temperature.

Indonesians sit on chairs or on grass mats while eating. Traditionally, they do not use forks or spoons. They eat with their right hand. The left hand, which is used for personal hygiene, is never used for eating.

appearance and ceremony, the tumpeng and its accessories presented a stimulating variety of natural, basic tastes: smooth coconut, salty fish, aromatic basil leaves, [and] hot chili.[17]

Religious Celebrations

Other celebrations are tied to religious holidays. Ninety percent of Indonesians are Muslim and for them **Ramadan** is the biggest religious celebration of the year. This month-long holiday falls at different times each year. During Ramadan Muslims typically fast from dawn to dusk in an effort to cleanse their souls. Fasting involves giving up all food and drink. Daily meals are limited to two: suhoor, a pre-dawn meal that starts the daily fast, and iftar, the evening meal that breaks it.

Iftar is usually a large meal in which everyone is welcome. Socializing and sharing is an important part of iftar. "Our doors are always open unless we are asleep," says Mariam, an Indonesian woman. "The idea is to share and share alike. If one neighbor hasn't cooked, it is only natural that another will share his or her iftar."[18]

The look, taste, and aroma of the food served at the iftar meal are also important. Although menus vary, most Indonesians break the fast with something sweet and fruity. Top choices are chopped fruit served with ice or kolak. This is a soupy dish made of bananas stewed in coconut milk. Palm sugar and vanilla-scented pandan

The iftar meal marks the end of the Ramadan fasting period.

Kolak

Kolak is a tasty treat that is not difficult to make. It can be served warm, chilled, or at room temperature.

Ingredients
4 firm bananas, cut into thick slices
1 can (14 ounces) coconut milk
1 ½ cups water
⅓ cup brown sugar
1 teaspoon vanilla extract
1 teaspoon cinnamon
Pinch salt

Directions
1. Combine all the ingredients except the bananas in a saucepan. Bring almost to a boil over medium heat. Immediately reduce heat to low or coconut milk will curdle.
2. Add the bananas. Simmer until the liquid thickens, stirring often.

Serves 4.

leaves are added as a flavoring. Some cooks throw in sweet potatoes, which gives the dish a bright color and extra sweetness. The mixture is slowly simmered until all the ingredients have soaked in the vanilla and coconut flavors. Kolak has a delicate taste and exotic fragrance. And, it is easy to digest on an empty stomach.

Kolak is sold by vendors all over Indonesia during Ramadan. According to Indonesian journalist Primastuti Handayani, "It's very easy to find people selling these sweet treats in traditional markets or even sidewalk food stalls. It's a seasonal business helpful enough

Spice Cake

This is a rich, sweet-smelling cake. It is buttery and moist, too.

Ingredients
2 cups flour
1 cup unsalted butter at room temperature
1 cup brown sugar
4 eggs
½ cup milk
1 teaspoon baking powder
¾ teaspoon baking soda
Pinch of salt
1 teaspoon each of nutmeg and ground ginger
1 tablespoon cinnamon
½ teaspoon ground cloves
1 teaspoon vanilla extract

Directions
1. Preheat the oven to 350°F.
2. Beat together the butter and sugar. Beat in the eggs, milk, and vanilla until the mixture is fluffy.
3. Combine the flour, baking soda, and spices. Add to the butter mixture. Mix well.
4. Spray a 9-inch tube or loaf pan with nonstick spray. Pour in the batter.
5. Bake for about 1 hour or until a fork inserted in the center of the cake comes away dry. Let the cake cool.

Makes one cake. Serves 12.

for office workers who may have to break their fast on their way home in Jakarta's suburbs … breaking the fast without kolak feels like that day is incomplete."[19]

Incredibly Fragrant

Spekkuk is another popular food of the iftar meal. It is an incredibly pretty and fragrant spice cake. This moist and golden masterpiece can be just a single layer or it can be up to twenty layers tall. Since Indonesians do not eat their meals in any particular order, the cake may be eaten alongside dishes like rice, fish, and sambal, or it may be eaten with a cup of tea at the close of the meal. Either way, it is sweet and yummy.

The Dutch, who ruled Indonesia for more than 300 years, introduced spice cake to the islands. Indonesian cooks were able to add to the cake the freshest, most sweet-smelling palm sugar, nutmeg, cloves, and cinnamon found anywhere. These ingredients made their spice cakes all the more flavorful and fragrant. Blogger Courtenay Beinhorn Dunk explains: "When I made this cake, I was fortunate to have a supply of nutmeg that grew in the Banda Islands [in Indonesia]. Most of the nutmeg consumed in America comes from the much closer island of Grenada. The nutmegs, encased in shiny brown hulls, are double the size of any I've seen before, and when freshly grated, their sweet, warm aroma is almost intoxicating…. I have never smelled a batter as fragrant as the one for this cake."[20]

Edible Art

Other beautiful and sweet-smelling foods are a part of religious festivals on the island of Bali. Most of the people are Hindus there. They believe their gods are everywhere and they choose to honor those gods in special ways. For example, the Balinese people place lovely little packets of woven banana leaves filled with rice all over the island as offerings to their gods. During religious festivals they create larger and fancier offerings, which can best be described as edible works of art. These are tall, brightly colored cone-shaped towers constructed of fruits, multicolored rice cakes, flowers, and little sweets perched on flat woven platters. Young women gracefully balance these on their heads as they parade to their local temples. There, the offerings are carried up staircases and placed on special platforms. The display of these cone-shaped food towers can number into the thousands. Once the offerings have been blessed, the worshippers take them apart and eat them, leaving choice morsels behind for the gods. Travel writer Marion Friedel describes what she saw when visiting Bali:

> A steep staircase leads to the sacred precinct [area]. In the center we see platforms on which are piled mountains of gifts, of fruit, colored rice cakes and flowers.... Over loudspeakers priests read sacred texts...and various groups, large and small, pray aloud. . . .

Indonesian Wildlife

Indonesia is home to a huge variety of animals and plants. Its jungles and rainforests contain many unique tropical plants, including a wide variety of orchids and plants that trap insects. Indonesia is also home to the world's largest flower, rafflesia. It measures about 39 inches (100cm) tall.

The world's largest lizard, the komodo dragon, also makes its home in Indonesia. It can measure 9.8 feet (3m) long. Tigers, leopards, orangutans, elephants, crocodiles, tree kangaroos, turtles, tortoises, and dozens of species of snakes and lizards are found there, too. There are also many different kinds of monkeys. One monkey known as a beruk is trained to climb tall palm trees and pick coconuts.

Thousands of different insect species live in Indonesia, including enormous butterflies. There are many colorful birds, too. Parrots, egrets, herons, and eagles are just a few.

Indonesia's rafflesia flower is the world's largest flower.

Balinese women walk in a procession, carrying offerings to the temple.

The festival lasts for five days and five nights. Over 200,000 people come with their ... gifts.... Over the five days, the visitors demolish [eat up] mountains of edible gifts, and even the gods are presented with little dishes of delicious tidbits. No one is allowed to go hungry.[21]

This is just one special way in which Indonesians celebrate life. Handwoven rice packets, vividly colored edible towers, golden rice cones, incredibly fragrant cakes, and sweet creamy fruit soups make holidays and special occasions a treat for all the senses.

Metric Conversions

Mass (weight)

1 ounce (oz.) = 28.0 grams (g)
8 ounces = 227.0 grams
1 pound (lb.)
    or 16 ounces = 0.45 kilograms (kg)
2.2 pounds = 1.0 kilogram

Liquid Volume

1 teaspoon (tsp.) = 5.0 milliliters (ml)
1 tablespoon (tbsp.) = 15.0 milliliters
1 fluid ounce (oz.) = 30.0 milliliters
1 cup (c.) = 240 milliliters
1 pint (pt.) = 480 milliliters
1 quart (qt.) = 0.96 liters (l)
1 gallon (gal.) = 3.84 liters

Pan Sizes

8-inch cake pan = 20 x 4-centimeter cake pan
9-inch cake pan = 23 x 3.5-centimeter cake pan
11 x 7-inch baking pan = 28 x 18-centimeter baking pan
13 x 9-inch baking pan = 32.5 x 23-centimeter baking pan
9 x 5-inch loaf pan = 23 x 13-centimeter loaf pan
2-quart casserole = 2-liter casserole

Temperature

212°F = 100°C (boiling point of water)
225°F = 110°C
250°F = 120°C
275°F = 135°C
300°F = 150°C
325°F = 160°C
350°F = 180°C
375°F = 190°C
400°F = 200°C

Length

1/4 inch (in.) = 0.6 centimeters (cm)
1/2 inch = 1.25 centimeters
1 inch = 2.5 centimeters

Notes

Chapter 1: A Special Place

1. John Oseland. *Cradle of Flavor.* New York: W.W. Norton, 2006, p. 95.

2. Quoted in John Oseland. *Cradle of Flavor,* p. 116.

3. Patrick Witton. *World Food Indonesia.* Victoria, Australia: Lonely Planet, 2002, p. 29.

4. Rafael Steinberg. *Pacific and Southeast Asian Cooking.* Alexandria, VA: Time-Life, 1970, p. 67.

5. Witton. *World Food Indonesia,* p. 39.

6. Oseland. *Cradle of Flavor,* p. 204.

Chapter 2: Unity in Diversity

7. Anthony Bourdain. "No Reservations: Indonesia." *Travel Channel,* 2006.

8. Bourdain. "No Reservations: Indonesia."

9. Quoted in Oseland. *Cradle of Flavor,* p. 140.

10. Quoted in Robin Eckhardt. "The Dish: Gado Gado." *Wall Street Journal,* August 29, 2008. http://online.wsj.com/article/SB121993992042780049.html.

Chapter 3: A Flavorful Adventure

11. Witton. *World Food Indonesia,* p. 175.

12. Quoted in Michele Kayal. "Capital Culture: Single Comment by Obama Sends Indonesia's National Street Food to Stardom." *Washington Examiner,* November 16, 2010. http://dev.www.washingtonexaminer.com/politics/ap/108425969.html.

13. Oseland. *Cradle of Flavor,* p. 340.

14. Bourdain. "No Reservations: Indonesia."

15. Pepy. "Jus Alpukat—Indonesian Avocado Blended/Shake," *Indonesian Eats*, May 20, 2010. http://indonesia-eats.blogspot.com/2010/05/jus-alpukat-indonesian-avocado.html.

Chapter 4: Beautiful Food

16. Bourdain. "No Reservations: Indonesia."

17. Steinberg. *Pacific and Southeast Asian Cooking,* p. 75.

18. Quoted in Somayya Jabarti. "Iftar—Different Cultures Have Different Dishes." *Arab News.* http://archive.arabnews.com/?page=9&section=0&article=35062&d=14&m=11&y=2003.

19. Primastuti Handayani. "By the Way: Ramadan is Not Just About 'Kolak' and Shopping." *Jakarta News*, August 23, 2009. www.thejakartapost.com/news/2009/08/23/by-way-ramadan-not-just-about-%E2%80%98kolak%E2%80%99-and-shopping.html.

20. Courtenay Beinhorn Dunk. "Recipe: From the Spice Islands, a Dutch Cake Fragrant with Nutmeg, Cinnamon and Clove." *SpiceLines*, February 11, 2007.

21. Marion Friedel. "Bali: The Island of Gods and Spirits." Michael Friedel Photo Library. www.foto-friedel.com/www_de/stories/FEATURE_BALI.php.

Glossary

archipelago: A group or chain of islands.

bumbu-bumbu: A paste made with ground spices and other flavorings.

coconut milk: A liquid made by mixing grated coconut with water.

condiment: Something added to food to improve its flavor, such as a seasoning or sauce.

coriander: A strongly scented parsley-like herb.

cumin: A spice with a bitter taste.

edible: Fit to be eaten.

kaki-limas: Three-wheeled snack carts that are pushed by vendors.

kecap manis: A popular sweet-salty sauce made with soy sauce and palm sugar.

palm sugar: A type of brown sugar made from the sap of palm trees.

Ramadan: A month-long religious holiday in which Muslims fast from dawn to dusk.

sambal: A spicy relish-like food that is served with Indonesian meals.

sauté: To lightly fry in a small amount of oil.

tempeh: Fermented soybeans.

tofu: A bland tasting food made by pressing bean curd into blocks.

warungs: Portable canvas-covered food stalls

For Further Exploration

Books

Lynda Cohen Cassanos. *Indonesia.* Broomall, PA: Mason Crest, 2010. Looks at Indonesia's geography, climate, history, relations with other countries, and the problems facing the country.

Robin Lim. *Indonesia.* Minneapolis: Lerner Classroom, 2010. This book takes readers on a tour of Indonesia, with information about the land, culture, people, food, flag, language, and capital.

Tamara Orr. *It's Cool to Learn About Countries: Indonesia.* Ann Arbor, MI: Cherry Lake, 2010. Information about Indonesia's geography, people, culture, and daily life.

Kayleen Reusser. *Recipe and Craft Guide to Indonesia.* Hockessin, DE: Mitchell Lane, 2010. This book contains Indonesian recipes and easy craft activities; with photos.

Websites

Central Intelligence Agency, "The World Factbook: Indonesia" (www.cia.gov/library/publications/the-world-factbook/geos/id.html). Provides a wealth of information about Indonesia's government, economy, challenges, land, and people.

Embassy of Indonesia, "Children's Page" (http://kids. embassyofindonesia.org/). This website created for kids gives information, maps, and pictures about life in Indonesia.

National Geographic, "Indonesia" (http://travel .nationalgeographic.com/travel/countries/indonesia-guide/). This website has beautiful photos, plus lots of facts, and a map.

Index

Picture Credits

Cover Photo: FoodPhotography Eising/StockFood Creative/Getty Images

Aaron Black/The Image Bank/Getty Images, 9

© Alistair Laming/Alamy, 35

AP Images/Larry Crowe, 33

© Bon Appetit/Alamy, 11

© Brian Leatart/the food passionates/Corbis, 26

© Edmund Lowe/Alamy, 10

© Eye Ubiquitous/Alamy, 31

© foodfolio/Alamy, 6

© IML Image Group Ltd/Alamy, 20

© Ingo Jezierski/Alamy, 28

© Laurie Strachan/Alamy, 18

Lianne Milton/The Image Bank/Getty Images, 12-13

Nicholas DeVore/Stone/Getty Images, 50-51

© Paul C. Pet/Corbis, 22

© paul kennedy/Alamy, 49

© Peter Netley/Alamy, 24

Romeo Gacad/AFP/Getty Images, 44

© Stewart Weir/Alamy, 37

© Stringer/Indonesia/Reuters/Corbis, 41

©Philip Game/Alamy, 30

About the Author

Barbara Sheen is the author of more than 70 books for young people. She lives in New Mexico with her family. In her spare time, she likes to swim, garden, read, and walk. Of course, she loves to cook!